MW00881366

4HOT-ty's

The Harmonious, Optimal, & Transformative Age.

DR. FLORENCE FASAN

TITLE: 4HOT-TY'S

SUB-TITLE: The Harmonious, Optimal & Transformative Age.

AUTHOR: Dr. Florence Fasan

ISBN-13: 9798335706650

Author's Preface

I was sure I had written all the literary work inside of me; after all, I had authored "The Aha Moment," "When Life Gives You Lemons," "Who Am I Without the World," "Boss Mode," and "The Intentional Woman." So, why did I write this newest book?

It all started with a chain of events and coincidences. I was browsing online and saw this lovely, fuchsia-colored outfit, and I was drawn to it particularly because it was my favorite color, at least for quite some time now. "This is going to be the outfit for your book cover," I heard a familiar voice say. I call that voice my fashion angel, who has been with me since I lost my fashion motivation and inspiration: my late mother. She always loved seeing me looking good, ensuring I was up to date on fashion trends that fit, not just because it was trending. I seriously believe I am drawn to certain styles, and when I get them, they are usually very intentionally selected by "us," I believe. LOL.

Book Cover! "Yeah, right," I said within. Days after, I started thinking about my birthday and wondered what I wanted to do. The usual way I celebrated was to go out with a few friends and/or travel somewhere for a relaxing vacation. After all, my birthday is usually after the Miss Elegance Georgia Pageant, a purpose-driven event that I founded to inspire and empower teen girls and young adult women, so it is always a good way for me to re-energize after a hectic preparation and eventually a successful event.

This next coincidence occurred one beautiful night as I lay in bed after a fulfilling and intentional day. I reflected on life thus far and appreciated that I had become wiser and more resilient in my 40s. I was proud of the woman I had become and excited to enter the next decade with all the knowledge, wisdom, and understanding. And aha, a compelling thought to write about the 40s, the decade when women start to embrace who they are and are more prepared for the journey ahead was birth.

I chose the color Orange for the cover and Pink for the outfit because I connected to the narrative on color psychology for book covers, a publication by LucidBooks that emphasizes that the most common emotion that orange evokes is excitement. This is because orange is a very stimulating color. It is also associated with happiness and fun. Therefore, when you see an orange book cover, it is likely that the book will be enjoyable to read. Pink helps attract readers looking for a particular type of story. In addition, pink is often used on book covers that feature female protagonists, as it is seen as a more traditionally "feminine" color.

As I embarked on this new literary endeavor, I realized that my previous works had laid the groundwork for this moment. Each book has been a stepping-stone, guiding me closer to the realization that the 40s is not just another decade but a period of being in harmony, optimal living, and transformation. While my previous books had touched on various aspects of personal growth and empowerment, "4HOT-ty 's holds a special significance. The abbreviation HOT stands for:

Harmonious: forming a pleasing or consistent whole.
Optimal: the best possible version of something.
Transformative: causing or able to cause an important and lasting change in someone or something.

The 40s is a time of immense change and transition. I want to highlight this remarkable decade. For those who may be navigating into their 40s, I want to prepare them for it and approach this stage of life with courage, curiosity, and an open heart. For those in their 40s, I want to empower them to embrace their experiences. For those in the next decade or more, I want to remind them of this Harmonious, Optimal, and Transformative age.

I am grateful and excited to invite you to embark on this journey with me. By sharing my insights and those of other women (names and exact circumstances have been changed for privacy), I aim to unveil the boundless possibilities in the 4HOT-TY'S and the transformative power of this decade.

I am so proud of the woman I have become.
I am grateful to God for the journey, experiences, and
people that have shaped me into who I am today.
~ Dr. Florence Fasan

Introduction

In life's journey, each decade offers its own set of challenges, triumphs, and revelations. Among these, the 40s stand as a unique threshold, a bridge between the exuberance of youth and the wisdom of maturity. It is an age marked by a subtle harmony, where your ambitions begin to harmonize with the symphony of self-awareness, where the pursuit of passion intertwines with the embrace of purpose.

Step into the world of 4HOT-ty's: Embracing Harmony, Optimal Living, and Transformation, a captivating journey into the heart of this remarkable decade. This book offers a unique perspective on the 40s, presenting it as a time of profound significance — when the seeds of past endeavors bloom into the fruits of wisdom, and the canvas of life eagerly awaits the brushstrokes of our aspirations.

It is a testament to the art of finding equilibrium amidst the complexities of modern existence—a delicate dance between ambition and contentment, between growth and acceptance. Through introspection and insight, uncover the keys to unlocking a life of serenity, purpose, and fulfillment.

The 40s represent the H.O.T. age for many individuals due to a convergence of factors contributing to personal and professional growth, fulfillment, and well-being. Here are some reasons why the 40s are often considered the H.O.T. age:

- The Blossoming of Self-Awareness
- The Epoch of Accumulated Wisdom
- Established Identity Unveiled
- Financial Stability and Independence
- The Pinnacle of Life Satisfaction
- Relationship Maturity
- Nurturing Friendships
- Parenting
- Godliness
- Authentic Self
- Embracing Serenity
- Physical and Mental Well-being
- Being Intentional

Contents

Chapter 1

The Blossoming of Self-Awareness

The Blossoming of Self-Awareness

"I Had So Many Aha Moments because I became Self Aware."

~ Sandra Grace, Life Coach.

Self-awareness, the ability to introspect and understand one's thoughts, feelings, and behaviors, is a cornerstone of personal growth and fulfillment. Women in their 40s often undergo a profound journey of self-discovery fueled by life experiences, introspection, and a deepening understanding of themselves.

A remarkable journey unfolds in a woman's 40s—the blossoming of self-awareness. This pivotal decade allows women to delve deep into their inner selves and discover layers of identity, purpose, and authenticity. As they navigate the complexities of midlife, women in their 40s embark on a transformative quest of self-discovery, embracing their strengths, acknowledging their vulnerabilities, and forging a deeper connection with their true essence.

At the heart of this journey lies a heightened sense of self-awareness—a keen understanding of one's values, beliefs, and aspirations. Women in their 40s embark on a voyage of self-exploration, peeling back the layers of societal expectations and cultural conditioning to uncover the essence of their true selves. They confront the narratives of their past, reclaiming ownership of their stories and rewriting the script of their lives with courage and conviction.

This period of self-awareness is characterized by a profound sense of empowerment—a recognition of one's inherent worth and potential. Women in their 40s embrace their uniqueness, celebrating their individuality and refusing to be confined by societal norms or expectations. They embrace their flaws and imperfections, viewing them not as shortcomings but as valuable lessons that contribute to their growth and evolution.

Self-awareness in the 40s is also synonymous with authenticity—a commitment to living in alignment with one's true self. Women embrace their authenticity, honoring their intuition and inner wisdom as guides on their journey. They cultivate a sense of integrity, refusing to compromise their values or sacrifice their authenticity for the sake of conformity or acceptance.

As women in their 40s deepen their self-awareness, they cultivate a profound sense of gratitude and acceptance. They embrace the full spectrum of human experience—the highs and lows, the triumphs and challenges—with grace and equanimity. They find beauty in the journey of self-discovery, recognizing that every experience, whether joyful or painful, contributes to their growth and evolution.

This period of self-awareness also brings with it a

heightened sense of purpose—a clarity of vision that guides women towards their true calling. They tap into their passions and talents, aligning their actions with their values and aspirations. They embark on new adventures, pursue meaningful endeavors, and make bold choices that reflect their authentic selves.

Self-awareness in the 40s is not just an individual journey but also a collective awakening—a recognition of the interconnectedness of all beings and the shared humanity that unites us. Women cultivate empathy and compassion, extending kindness and understanding to themselves and others. They forge deeper connections with loved ones, fostering intimacy and authenticity in their relationships.

As women in their 40s embrace the blossoming of self-awareness, they emerge with a newfound sense of resilience and inner strength. They navigate life's challenges with grace and courage, drawing upon their self-awareness as a source of guidance and empowerment. They embrace change as a natural part of the journey, trusting in their ability to adapt and thrive in the face of adversity.

In essence, the 40s herald a profound awakening—a time of self-discovery, growth, and transformation. As women embrace the blossoming of self-awareness, they step into their power, reclaiming their authenticity, and embracing the fullness of who they are. It is a journey of empowerment, purpose, and fulfillment.

Edith's Story

Edith, a woman in her 40s, had spent much of her life tending to the needs of others. As a devoted wife, mother, and career woman, she had always put the needs of her family and job before her own. Edith began to feel a stirring within her—a longing to explore her own desires and aspirations and to embark on a journey of self-discovery.

It started with small moments of introspection, as Edith found herself questioning the meaning and purpose of her life. She realized that she had spent so much time focusing on fulfilling the expectations of others that she had neglected her own dreams and passions. And so, with a newfound determination, she set out to uncover the depths of her true self.

As Edith delved into the depths of her soul, she unearthed layers of hidden desires and long-forgotten dreams. She discovered a love for painting, a passion for writing, and a deep yearning for connection with nature. These revelations ignited a spark within her—a spark of self-awareness that illuminated the path to her true essence.

With each stroke of her paintbrush and every word she penned, Edith felt herself coming alive in ways she had never experienced before. She found solace in the creative process, using art and writing as a means of expression and self-discovery. Through these mediums, she explored her innermost thoughts and feelings, unraveling the mysteries of her soul one brushstroke at a time. But self-awareness was not just about uncovering hidden talents and passions; it was also about confronting the parts of herself she had long ignored. Edith confronted her fears and insecurities head-on, embracing her vulnerabilities as an integral part of her journey towards self-acceptance. She learned to love herself fully, flaws and all, recognizing that true authenticity lay in embracing every aspect of her being.

As Edith's self-awareness blossomed, so too did her relationships with others. She found herself approaching interactions with a newfound sense of empathy and compassion, understanding that everyone was on their own journey of self-discovery. She listened more deeply, spoke more honestly, and connected more authentically with those around her.

In her 40s, Edith's blossoming self-awareness became a guiding light, illuminating the path to a life of fulfillment and purpose. She embraced her true self with open arms, knowing that her journey towards self-discovery was far from over. And as she stepped into the fullness of who she was meant to be, Edith radiated a sense of peace and contentment that touched everyone she encountered.

How Women in their 40's can Foster Self-Awareness

Women in their 40s can foster self-awareness through

various practices and strategies that encourage introspection, reflection, and personal growth. Here are some ways they can do so:

1. Engage in Self-Reflection: Allocate time for self-reflection regularly. This can involve journaling, meditation, or simply quiet contemplation to explore thoughts, feelings, and experiences.

2. Embrace Feedback: Seek feedback from trusted friends, family members, or mentors. Constructive feedback offers valuable insights into blind spots or areas for growth and fosters self-awareness.

3. Explore Personal Values and Beliefs: Examine core values and beliefs to understand what truly matters. This exploration helps align actions and decisions with authentic selves.

4. Practice Mindfulness: Engage in mindfulness techniques such as meditation, deep breathing, or body scans. Mindfulness cultivates present-moment awareness, allowing observation of thoughts and emotions without judgment.

5. Explore Emotional Intelligence: Develop emotional intelligence by recognizing and understanding your own emotions and those of others. Learn to label emotions accurately and regulate them effectively.

6. Seek New Experiences: Step outside your comfort zone and try new activities or experiences. Novel experiences provide opportunities for self-discovery and growth, expanding self-awareness.

7. Embrace Vulnerability: Create a safe and supportive environment where vulnerability is welcomed. Encourage open and honest communication about fears, insecurities, and challenges to foster deeper self-awareness and connection.

8. Reflect on Past Experiences: Reflect on past experiences and lessons learned. Identify patterns or themes in lives and understand how past experiences have shaped who they are today.

9. Practice Self-Compassion: Be kind and compassionate toward yourself, especially during times of struggle or difficulty. Treat yourself with the same kindness and understanding as you would offer to a friend.

10. Set Intentions and Goals: Set intentions and goals that align with values and aspirations. Clear intentions provide direction and purpose, guiding the journey of self-awareness and personal growth.

By embracing these practices and strategies, women in their 40s can cultivate greater self-awareness, leading to a deeper understanding of themselves and their place in the world.

In conclusion, women in their 40s embark on a profound journey of self-awareness, embracing their authentic selves, cultivating emotional intelligence, and prioritizing personal growth and self-care. Through introspection, empathy, and a commitment to authenticity, women navigate life's complexities with grace, resilience, and a deep sense of purpose. As they continue to unfold the layers of self-discovery, they embrace the richness of their inner worlds, finding fulfillment and empowerment in their journey of self-awareness and self-actualization.

Chapter 2

The Epoch of Accumulated Wisdom

The Epoch of Accumulated Wisdom

Wisdom is not inherited; it's cultivated through a lifetime of learning, experiencing, and reflecting.

~ Dr. Florence Fasan, Serial Entrepreneur

The 40s is a pivotal chapter where the seeds of experience blossom into the fruits of wisdom. It is a time when the cumulative lessons of the past converge to illuminate the path forward, guiding women through the intricacies of relationships, careers, health, and self-discovery. In this chapter, we delve into the profound reservoir of accumulated wisdom accompanying the journey through the 40s, exploring how it shapes perceptions, choices, and, ultimately, the course of life itself.

As individuals navigate their 40s, they find themselves drawing upon the wellspring of their past experiences, both joyful and challenging, to inform their present decisions and shape their future aspirations. They have walked the winding paths of youth and weathered the storms of early adulthood, emerging stronger, wiser, and more resilient with each step taken. The 40s offer a precious opportunity to reflect upon these experiences, to distill their essence into valuable insights, and to integrate them into the fabric of one's being.

This decade is characterized by increased self-awareness, confidence, and a deeper understanding of oneself and the world. It is during this time that many women accumulate wisdom and gain invaluable insights that shape their lives moving forward. Armed with a deeper understanding of themselves and the world, they become catalysts for change — inspiring others, effecting meaningful transformations, and leaving a lasting legacy that extends far beyond the confines of their own lives.

One of the most notable aspects of wisdom gained in the 40s is a heightened sense of self-acceptance and self-love. Women in their 40s often recognize and embrace their strengths, weaknesses, and imperfections, understanding that these qualities contribute to their unique identity. They learn to prioritize self-care and prioritize their own happiness above societal expectations or pleasing others. This newfound wisdom enables them to set healthier boundaries, let go of toxic relationships, and make choices that align with their own values and aspirations.

Another essential aspect of wisdom gained in the 40s is a deeper understanding of personal goals and desires. Women reach a stage where they reflect on their past achievements, evaluate their current situations, and ponder upon their future aspirations. They realize the importance of aligning their actions and decisions with their long-term objectives, be it personal or professional. This clarity empowers them to pursue their passions unapologetically and take calculated risks necessary to reach their full potential.

Furthermore, women in their 40s often develop a more profound sense of empathy and compassion. Having experienced various life challenges and gained insights from their own struggles, they become more understanding and accepting of others' journeys. They develop the wisdom to recognize that everyone has their battles and that kindness and compassion can go a long way in fostering connections and building a supportive community.

Additionally, the 40s bring a sense of liberation and a shift towards embracing authenticity. Many women have spent their earlier years conforming to societal norms and expectations. However, as they approach this stage of life, they feel a growing need to be true to themselves. They let go of the need for external validation and embrace their unique qualities, quirks, and beliefs. This wisdom allows women to express their voices, share their stories, and inspire others with their authenticity.

In essence, the 40s is a time to celebrate the richness of life's experiences, to embrace the journey of personal evolution, and to revel in the beauty of the era of accumulated wisdom.

Lastly, wisdom gained in the 40s often includes a deeper appreciation for the present moment and a sense of gratitude. Having weathered several of life's storms, women understand the transformative power of gratitude. Women become more attuned to the beauty and joy in their everyday lives, whether it be simple pleasures, meaningful connections, or fulfilling experiences. This wisdom allows them to savor life's precious moments and find contentment in the present, regardless of external circumstances.

May's Story

May was a woman in her 40s, whose journey through life had gifted her with a treasure trove of accumulated wisdom. Born and raised in a small town, she had always possessed a quiet strength and a keen sense of observation that allowed her to glean insights from every experience.

In her twenties, May pursued her dreams with fervor, eager to carve out a path of her own. She faced challenges and setbacks along the way, but each obstacle only served to deepen her resilience and determination. Through hard work and perseverance, she had built a successful career in marketing, earning the respect of her colleagues and clients alike.

As she entered her thirties, May found herself confronting the complexities of love and relationships. She experienced heartbreak and disappointment, but she refused to let them define her. Instead, she embraced the lessons learned from each failed romance, recognizing the importance of self-love and authenticity in building meaningful connections.

In her 40s, May's wisdom blossomed like never before.

She had weathered the storms of life and emerged stronger and wiser than ever. She approached each day with a sense of gratitude and humility, knowing that every experience held the potential for growth and enlightenment.

May's accumulated wisdom guided her through both triumphs and tribulations. When faced with difficult decisions, she relied on her intuition and inner wisdom to light the way forward. She understood the power of empathy and compassion, reaching out to others with a listening ear and a caring heart.

Despite the inevitable challenges that life threw her way, May remained steadfast in her belief in the inherent goodness of humanity. She approached each interaction with kindness and understanding, knowing that true wisdom lay in seeing the beauty and potential in every soul she encountered.

As May journeyed through her 40s, she continued to embrace the wonders of life with childlike wonder and curiosity. She found joy in simple pleasures and took delight in the beauty of nature. She savored each moment, knowing that life was a precious gift to be cherished and celebrated.

May's accumulated wisdom had transformed her into a beacon of light and inspiration for those around her. Her presence radiated warmth and wisdom, and her words carried the weight of a lifetime of experiences. She had learned that wisdom could only be learned through living fully and embracing the richness of life in all its glory. And as she looked towards the future, May did so with a heart full of gratitude and a soul ablaze with wisdom.

How to Foster the Use of Accumulated Wisdom

Fostering the use of accumulated wisdom involves cultivating a mindset of continuous learning, reflection, and application of insights gained from life experiences. Here are several strategies to foster the use of your accumulated wisdom:

1. Reflect Regularly: Set aside time regularly for introspection and reflection on your experiences, decisions, and lessons learned. Journaling, meditation, or quiet contemplation can help you gain clarity and insights into your thoughts and actions.

2. Seek Feedback: Be open to receiving feedback from others, whether it's from mentors, peers, or loved ones. Constructive feedback can provide valuable perspectives and insights that help you refine your thinking and behavior.

3. Mentor Others: Share your knowledge, experiences, and lessons learned with others by mentoring or coaching individuals who can profit from your wisdom. Serving as a mentor not only helps others but also reinforces your own

understanding and application of your accumulated wisdom.

4. Set Goals: Based on your values, priorities, and aspirations, set specific, achievable goals. Use your accumulated wisdom to inform your goal-setting process, identifying areas where you can apply past lessons to achieve desired outcomes.

5. Embrace Challenges: View challenges and setbacks as opportunities for growth and learning rather than obstacles to be avoided. Draw upon your accumulated wisdom to navigate challenges with resilience, creativity, and adaptability.

6. Practice Gratitude: Cultivate gratitude for the experiences, relationships, and opportunities that have contributed to your accumulated wisdom. Acknowledge and appreciate the lessons learned from both successes and failures, recognizing their role in shaping who you are today.

7. Stay Curious: Maintain a lifelong curiosity and thirst for knowledge, exploring new ideas, perspectives, and experiences. Keep an open mind and be willing to question assumptions, challenge beliefs, and seek out diverse viewpoints to expand your understanding of the world.

8. Take Action: Apply your accumulated wisdom by taking purposeful action aligned with your values and goals. Use

past experiences and insights to inform your decisions,

In conclusion, women in their 40s often possess a wealth of accumulated wisdom derived from their varied life experiences. This wisdom is characterized by a deep understanding of themselves and their values, enhanced emotional intelligence, and resilience built from overcoming challenges. They have learned the importance of self-care, balance, and healthy personal and professional boundaries. A greater appreciation often marks their insights for authenticity, meaningful connections, and the ability to navigate life's complexities with grace and confidence. This period of life sees them embracing growth, self-acceptance, and a clearer sense of purpose, allowing them to contribute thoughtfully to their communities and inspire others through their lived experiences.

Chapter 3

Established Identity Unveiled

Established Identity Unveiled

I can confidently look in the mirror and say this is who I am.

~ Dr. Daniela Peel

Women in their 40s typically have a clearer sense of self-identity and purpose. They have had time to explore different aspects of themselves and better understand their values, goals, and priorities, allowing them to make choices that align more closely with their authentic selves.

Self-Discovery and Exploration

The 40s marks a significant milestone in the journey of self-discovery. By this stage in life, individuals have accumulated a wealth of life experiences, both triumphs and setbacks, which contribute to a deeper understanding of themselves. They have had the opportunity to explore different roles, relationships, and interests, gaining insights into what truly resonates with their authentic selves. Whether through career paths, personal relationships, or creative pursuits, the 40s offer a fertile ground for self-exploration and growth.

Clarity of Values and Priorities

As women progress through their 40s, they often gain clarity regarding their core values and priorities. They have had time to reflect on what matters most and discern their true passions and aspirations.

This clarity enables them to make decisions that are more aligned with their authentic selves, whether in their careers, relationships, or lifestyle choices. By prioritizing what truly matters to them, individuals in their 40s can cultivate a sense of purpose and fulfillment that extends beyond external achievements or societal expectations.

Alignment of Goals and Actions

With a clearer sense of self-identity and purpose, individuals in their 40s are better equipped to align their goals and actions with their authentic selves. They have a deeper understanding of their strengths, weaknesses, and areas for growth, which enables them to set meaningful and achievable goals. Whether pursuing career advancement, personal development, or creative endeavors, individuals in their 40s are more intentional in their pursuits, focusing on what brings them joy, fulfillment, and a sense of purpose.

Authentic Living

Perhaps most importantly, the 40s are a time when individuals strive for authenticity in all aspects of their lives. They embrace their unique qualities, quirks, and imperfections, recognizing that true fulfillment comes from living in alignment with their authentic selves. Whether in their relationships, work, or personal endeavors, individuals in their 40s prioritize authenticity over conformity, choosing to express themselves openly and honestly, even if it means taking risks or challenging societal norms. The 40s offer a fertile ground for self-exploration and growth.

Juliet's Story

Juliet had always been a driven woman. In her 20s, she pursued her career in corporate law with unwavering determination. Her 30s were marked by the balancing act of building a family and climbing the corporate ladder. But it was in her 40s that Juliet truly began to live her life authentically, embracing her accumulated wisdom and stepping into her true self.

Juliet's journey towards authenticity began on her 40th birthday. Surrounded by friends and family, she felt a sudden clarity. Reflecting on the past decades, she realized that while she had achieved much, she had often suppressed her true desires and passions in favor of what was expected of her. That night, she made a promise to herself: the coming years would be different. She would live for herself, unapologetically and authentically.

The first step in Juliet's transformation was reconnecting with her passions. As a child, she had loved painting, but the demands of adulthood had left her little time for creative pursuits. She dusted off her old easel and began to paint again, finding joy and fulfillment in the strokes of her brush. Her artwork became a form of therapy, allowing her to express emotions and thoughts she had long suppressed.

Juliet also began to reassess her career. While she was successful, the corporate world no longer ignited her spirit. With careful consideration, she decided to transition into legal consulting, a role that allowed her more flexibility and the opportunity to mentor young women in the legal field. This change not only aligned with her professional expertise but also fulfilled her desire to make a meaningful impact.

In her personal life, Juliet embraced vulnerability and authenticity in her relationships. She had always been the strong one, the one people leaned on. But she realized that true strength also meant being open about her own struggles and fears. She started having deeper, more honest conversations with her husband, friends, and children. This openness strengthened her bonds, fostering a sense of intimacy and trust that she had never experienced before.

Self-care became a non-negotiable part of Juliet's life. She began practicing yoga and meditation, which helped her stay grounded and centered. She made time for regular walks in nature, savoring the simple pleasure of being outdoors. Juliet also prioritized her health, making mindful choices about her diet and ensuring she got enough rest.

As she embraced her authentic self, Juliet found that her confidence grew. She no longer felt the need to conform to societal expectations or seek approval from others. Instead, she trusted her intuition and made decisions that resonated with her true self. This newfound confidence was evident in every aspect of her life, from her personal style to the way she carried herself in professional settings.

Juliet's journey was not without challenges. There were moments of doubt and fear, times when she questioned her choices. But she learned to navigate these moments gracefully, using them as opportunities for growth and self-reflection. Each challenge she faced reinforced her commitment to living authentically.

One of the most rewarding aspects of Juliet's transformation was the inspiration she provided to others. Her friends and colleagues noticed her positive changes and began to seek her advice on how to live more authentically. Juliet became a mentor and role model, sharing her journey and encouraging others to embrace their true selves.

By her late 40s, Juliet felt a profound sense of fulfillment and contentment. She had created a life that was true to her values, passions, and aspirations. Living authentically had brought her joy, peace, and a deep sense of purpose. Juliet's story was a testament to the power of self-awareness, courage, and the unwavering pursuit of one's true self.

How to Foster an Established Identity

Establishing identity in your 40s is a multi-faceted journey that involves self-discovery, self-acceptance, and intentional growth. It's a time when accumulated life experiences, personal values, and aspirations converge to shape a strong sense of self. Here are some key aspects of establishing identity in your 40s:

1. Self-Reflection: The 40s often bring deeper self-awareness and introspection. Take time to reflect on your life journey, values, beliefs, strengths, and areas for growth. Consider the experiences that have shaped you and how they align with your authentic self.

2. Clarifying Values and Priorities: Identify your core values and priorities in life. What matters most to you? What are your non-negotiables? Use these values as a compass to guide your decisions, actions, and relationships.

3. Embracing Authenticity: In your 40s, there's a growing acceptance of who you truly are, flaws and all. Embrace your authenticity and celebrate your uniqueness. Let go of the need to conform to societal expectations or others' perceptions of who you should be.

4. Pursuing Passions and Purpose: Explore your passions and interests and consider how you can align them with your sense of purpose. Whether it's through work, hobbies, or community involvement, pursue activities that bring meaning and fulfillment to your life.

5. Setting Boundaries: Establish healthy boundaries in your relationships and commitments. Learn to say no to things

that drain your energy or don't align with your values. Prioritize your well-being and invest your time and resources in what truly matters to you.

6. Embracing Change: 40s often bring significant life transitions, such as career changes, empty nesting, or caring for aging parents. Embrace these changes as opportunities for growth and reinvention. Stay open to new possibilities and be willing to adapt to evolving circumstances.

7. Cultivating Resilience: Develop resilience in the face of adversity and challenges. Draw upon your past experiences to navigate setbacks with grace and determination. Trust in your ability to overcome obstacles and emerge stronger on the other side.

8. Nurturing Relationships: Cultivate meaningful connections with others who support and uplift you. Surround yourself with people who celebrate your authenticity and encourage your personal growth. Invest in nurturing relationships that bring joy, companionship, and mutual respect.

9. Finding Balance: Strive for balance in all areas of your life — work, family, health, and leisure. Prioritize self-care and well-being to maintain physical, emotional, and mental health. Seek harmony between your professional and personal pursuits to live a fulfilling and purpose-driven life.

10. Embracing Growth: Stay committed to lifelong learning and growth. Be open to new experiences, perspectives, and opportunities for self-improvement. Cultivate a growth mindset that embraces challenges as opportunities for learning and development.

In conclusion, the 40s represent a time of established identity, where individuals have a clearer sense of self-identity and purpose. Through self-discovery, exploration, and reflection, they have gained insights into their values, goals, and priorities, allowing them to make choices that align more closely with their authentic selves. By embracing authenticity and living with intention, individuals in their 40s can cultivate a sense of purpose, fulfillment, and joy that permeates every aspect of their lives.

Chapter 4

Chapter 4: Financial Stability and Independence

Financial Stability and Independence

My Money is working for me,

~ Deliqua Isom

Financial independence is a crucial aspect of a woman's life, and the 40s can be a turning point where women strive to achieve this goal. This period is often characterized by increased stability, personal growth, and the realization of long-term financial aspirations. Through various experiences and milestones, women in their 40s can gain financial wisdom and strive for independence.

One significant aspect of financial independence in the 40s is the ability to take control of personal finances. Many women reach this stage with a clearer understanding of their financial goals and priorities. They recognize the importance of budgeting, saving, and investing wisely to secure their financial future. During this time, they may take steps to pay off debts, build emergency funds, and develop a comprehensive financial plan, providing a sense of security and freedom to pursue their goals and aspirations.

Another important aspect is career advancement and achieving financial stability. In their 40s, women often have several years of experience in their respective fields, allowing them to progress in their careers and potentially earn higher incomes. They may consider seeking promotions, switching jobs for better opportunities, or exploring entrepreneurial endeavors. This pursuit of professional growth directly contributes to their financial independence and offers a sense of empowerment.

Additionally, women in their 40s understand the value of long-term financial planning. They recognize the significance of retirement savings and begin to focus on building a substantial nest egg. By leveraging retirement accounts, such as 401(k)s or IRAs, they actively contribute towards their financial security during their later years. They may also seek financial advisors' guidance to ensure they make the most prudent decisions regarding investments and financial strategies.

Furthermore, the 40s can be a time of clarity and reflection regarding financial priorities. Women may reassess their financial goals, separating needs from wants and aligning their spending habits accordingly. They become more adept at making sound financial choices, avoiding unnecessary debts, and setting realistic goals for themselves and their families.

Additionally, women in their 40s often prioritize financial literacy and education. They actively seek out resources and information to enhance their financial knowledge, empowering themselves to make informed decisions about investments, savings, and other financial matters. By understanding financial concepts and tools, they can navigate the often complex financial landscape with confidence and independence.

Lastly, financial independence in the 40s can also involve inspiring and mentoring younger women. These women often serve as role models, sharing their experiences and insights to empower others to take control of their finances. They actively contribute to women's collective progress and societal empowerment by encouraging financial responsibility and independence.

In conclusion, financial independence in women in their 40s is a multi-faceted journey encompassing various aspects of personal growth, career advancement, and financial planning. Through increased self-awareness, prudent decision-making, and a focus on long-term financial goals, women in their 40s can attain the financial stability and independence they aspire to. This empowers them individually and contributes to the collective progress of gender equality and financial well-being for women.

SMART FINANCIAL DECISIONS TO MAKE IN YOUR 40's

Making smart financial decisions in your 40s is crucial for securing your financial future and achieving long-term stability and prosperity. Here are some key strategies to consider:

1. Increase Retirement Savings: Retirement may seem distant in your 40s, but it's essential to prioritize saving

2. Pay Down Debt: Focus on paying off high-interest debt, such as credit card balances and personal loans. Reducing debt saves you money on interest, improves your overall financial health, and frees up resources for savings and investments.

3. Diversify Investments: Review your investment portfolio and ensure it's diversified across asset classes, such as stocks, bonds, and real estate. Consider your risk tolerance and investment goals when adjusting your allocation. Seek professional advice if needed to optimize your investment strategy.

4. Build Emergency Savings: Establish or bolster an emergency fund to cover unexpected expenses like medical bills or home repairs. Aim to save three to six months' worth of living expenses in a liquid, accessible account to provide financial security during unforeseen circumstances.

5. Review Insurance Coverage: Assess your insurance needs and ensure you have adequate coverage for health, life, disability, and property. Consider increasing coverage amounts as your financial responsibilities and assets grow. Shop around for competitive rates to maximize cost-effectiveness.

6. Plan for Children's Education: If you have children and have not started saving for their education expenses, such as college tuition, early to take advantage of compound

interest, consider tax-advantaged college savings accounts like 529 plans or Coverdell ESAs to maximize savings growth and minimize tax implications.

7. Create a Will and Estate Plan: Establish a comprehensive estate plan to protect and distribute your assets according to your wishes. Create a will, designate beneficiaries, and consider setting up trusts to manage assets and minimize estate taxes. Review and update your plan periodically to reflect any life changes.

8. Invest in Yourself: Continue to invest in your professional development and skills enhancement to remain competitive in the job market and increase your earning potential. Consider pursuing advanced education, certifications, or training opportunities that align with your career goals and interests.

9. Plan for Long-Term Care: Start planning for potential long-term care needs in your later years by exploring options such as long-term care insurance or setting aside funds for future care expenses. Research available resources and consult with a financial advisor to develop a personalized plan based on your circumstances.

10. Prioritize Quality of Life: While financial security is essential, remember to prioritize your overall quality of life. Allocate resources towards experiences, hobbies, and activities that bring joy and fulfillment to you and your

loved ones. Strive for a balanced approach to financial planning that considers both short-term enjoyment and long-term security.

By implementing these smart financial decisions in your 40s, you can set yourself on a path toward greater financial stability, security, and prosperity in the years ahead. Remember to regularly reassess your goals and adjust your financial plan as needed to adapt to changing circumstances and priorities.

Maria's Story

Maria Martinez grew up in a modest household. Her parents worked hard to make ends meet, instilling in her the values of perseverance and education. Maria excelled in school and eventually earned a scholarship to attend a prestigious university. After graduation, she landed a job in marketing, where she steadily climbed the corporate ladder.

Despite her professional success, Maria faced financial challenges in her 30s. She was burdened by student loans, a mortgage, and the expenses of raising two children as a single mother. Determined to achieve financial stability, she began educating herself about personal finance. She read books, attended seminars, and even took online courses on budgeting, investing, and retirement planning.

In her early 40s, Maria made a pivotal decision: she took a

risk and started her own marketing consulting firm. The first few years were tough, with long hours and unpredictable income, but her dedication paid off. By leveraging her extensive network and reputation in the industry, Maria's business began to thrive.

By the time she turned 45, Maria had paid off her student loans and built a substantial emergency fund and investment portfolio. She purchased a rental property that provided additional income and secured her children's college funds. Maria felt a profound sense of independence and security with her bright financial future.

Beyond her personal achievements, Maria became passionate about helping other women achieve financial independence. She started a blog to share her journey and financial tips and volunteered to teach financial literacy workshops at local community centers.

Maria's 40s became a decade of transformation. She embraced her newfound stability and independence, finding joy and fulfillment in her own success and empowering others to achieve their financial goals. Her story is a testament to the power of perseverance, education, and the courage to take risks for a better future.

Chapter 5

The Pinnacle of Life Satisfaction

The Pinnacle Of Life Satisfaction

"Your 40s are the best decade. If you've worked hard, done the right things, and been kind, your life is your reward. You're wiser, more at peace, and more comfortable in your skin than ever before." ~ Oprah Winfrey

Research has shown that overall life satisfaction tends to peak in the 40s. This may be due to a combination of factors, including increased self-awareness, greater financial stability, stronger social connections, and a sense of accomplishment and fulfillment in both personal and professional pursuits. For women in their 40s, life satisfaction encompasses a tapestry of experiences, relationships, and personal fulfillment. Navigating career advancement, relationship dynamics, health, and well-being, they cultivate resilience, authenticity, and a sense of purpose. Through self-reflection, growth, and the pursuit of passion, women in their 40s embrace the richness of life, finding fulfillment in their journeys of self-discovery and self-actualization.

Life satisfaction is a multifaceted construct influenced by various factors such as career, relationships, health, and personal fulfillment. For women in their 40s, this stage often represents a time of reflection, growth, and reevaluation of priorities.

CAREER PROGRESSION

Women in their 40s find themselves standing at the pinnacle of their careers, having ascended the ranks through a combination of dedication, perseverance, and skill. This stage of life often represents a culmination of years of hard work and experience, marked by notable career milestones that reflect their commitment to professional growth and advancement.

For some, these milestones come in the form of promotions within their current organizations, a testament to their expertise, leadership abilities, and contributions to the success of their teams. Whether climbing the corporate ladder or assuming leadership roles, women in their 40s demonstrate a strategic thinking, decision-making, and problem-solving capacity that sets them apart in their respective fields.

Others may choose to embark on entrepreneurial ventures, leveraging their expertise and experience to launch businesses or startups. The 40s offer a unique opportunity for women to pursue their entrepreneurial ambitions, armed with a wealth of industry knowledge, networks, and skills honed over the years. Whether founding their own companies or joining forces with like-minded entrepreneurs, women in their 40s exhibit a spirit of innovation, creativity, and resilience as they navigate the challenges and opportunities of entrepreneurship.

Additionally, many women in their 40s prioritize ongoing skill development and professional growth, recognizing the importance of staying abreast of industry trends and advancements. Whether through formal education, certifications, or professional development programs, they invest in themselves to remain competitive in an ever-evolving job market. By acquiring new skills, expanding their knowledge base, and adapting to emerging technologies, women in their 40s demonstrate a commitment to lifelong learning and excellence in their chosen fields.

WORK-LIFE BALANCE

In the 40s, women embark on a quest for equilibrium between their professional aspirations and personal obligations, a journey defined by the pursuit of work-life balance. This pivotal period signifies a conscious effort to prioritize self-care and well-being amidst the demands of career advancement and familial responsibilities. Recognizing that genuine satisfaction stems from achieving harmony between work and life domains, women in their 40s navigate this delicate balance with intention and purpose.

Amidst the bustling landscape of career pursuits, women in their 40s embark on a quest for fulfillment that transcends professional accolades alone. While they remain dedicated to their career trajectories and professional growth, they understand the importance of carving out time for personal fulfillment and emotional well-being. Whether through mindfulness practices, regular exercise routines, or moments of quiet reflection, they prioritize self-care as a cornerstone of their daily routines, recognizing that true success encompasses both professional achievements and personal fulfillment.

Simultaneously, women in their 40s recognize the significance of nurturing meaningful relationships and connections outside the workplace. As they strive to advance their careers, they also invest time and energy into cultivating strong bonds with family members, friends, and loved ones. Whether it's sharing quality time with their children, enjoying leisure activities with their partners, or fostering deep friendships, they understand that true satisfaction arises from the richness of their relationships and the depth of their connections.

Moreover, women in their 40s approach the pursuit of work-life balance with a profound sense of self-awareness and authenticity. They honor their individual needs and boundaries, advocate for their well-being, and prioritize activities that bring them joy and fulfillment. By aligning their actions with their values and aspirations, they create a sense of harmony and fulfillment that permeates every aspect of their lives.

In essence, the 40s represent a transformative period where women actively seek to integrate their professional aspirations with their personal values and priorities. By prioritizing self-care, nurturing meaningful relationships, and embracing authenticity, they embark on a journey towards achieving a harmonious balance between work and life—a journey that ultimately leads to a deeper sense of satisfaction and fulfillment.

RELATIONSHIP DYNAMICS AND EMOTIONAL WELL-BEING

In their 40s, women embark on a multifaceted journey in navigating relationship dynamics, a pivotal aspect of their emotional well-being and overall life satisfaction. This stage of life often finds women in various relationship statuses, from marriage and partnership to singlehood, each presenting its own set of challenges and rewards. Regardless of their relationship status, the cornerstone of healthy relationship dynamics lies in cultivating self-acceptance and self-love.

Self-acceptance is a powerful catalyst for fostering healthy relationships with themselves and others. Embracing their strengths, flaws, and unique attributes allows women to approach relationships from a place of authenticity and vulnerability, laying the foundation for genuine connections and meaningful interactions. This self-acceptance empowers women to set boundaries, communicate their needs, and navigate the complexities of interpersonal dynamics with confidence and grace.

Moreover, self-love is paramount in nurturing emotional well-being and resilience amidst the ebbs and flows of relationship dynamics. Women in their 40s prioritize self-care practices that honor their physical, emotional, and spiritual needs, recognizing that true fulfillment begins with a deep sense of self-worth and compassion.

By prioritizing their own well-being, they cultivate the inner strength and resilience needed to navigate the challenges and joys of relationships with grace and integrity.

In addition to self-acceptance and self-love, women in their 40s rely on close friendships and support networks as pillars of emotional support and companionship. These connections serve as sources of understanding, empathy, and validation, enriching women's lives and bolstering their sense of belonging. Whether sharing laughter and camaraderie with lifelong friends or seeking solace and advice from trusted confidants, women draw strength from the bonds of sisterhood and solidarity that enrich their lives immeasurably.

Furthermore, relationships with family members play a significant role in shaping women's overall life satisfaction and sense of identity. Whether nurturing bonds with children, parents, or siblings, these familial connections provide a sense of belonging and rootedness that anchors women amidst life's uncertainties. From celebrating milestones and triumphs to weathering challenges and setbacks, family relationships contribute to women's resilience and sense of purpose, shaping their sense of identity and connection in profound ways.

WELLNESS PRACTICES

Women in their 40s prioritize holistic wellness practices that encompass physical, mental, and emotional well-being, recognizing the profound impact of these practices on their vitality and longevity. This stage of life brings a heightened awareness of the importance of self-care and preventive healthcare, prompting women to adopt proactive measures to maintain their overall health and well-being.

Physical health takes precedence as women prioritize regular exercise, balanced nutrition, and preventive healthcare as essential components of their wellness routines. Through regular physical activity, whether through cardiovascular exercises, strength training, or yoga, women in their 40s enhance their physical fitness and boost their mood, energy levels, and overall well-being. Additionally, they prioritize balanced nutrition, fueling their bodies with nourishing foods rich in vitamins, minerals, and antioxidants to support optimal health and vitality. Preventive healthcare measures such as regular screenings, vaccinations, and check-ups are also prioritized to detect and address potential health issues before they escalate, empowering women to take proactive control of their health and well-being.

By incorporating these stress management practices into

their daily routines, women strengthen their ability to cope with stress, enhance their emotional resilience, and foster a sense of calm and tranquility amidst life's challenges.

Furthermore, self-care emerges as a cornerstone of women's overall well-being and life satisfaction in their 40s. Engaging in hobbies, creative pursuits, and activities that bring joy and fulfillment not only provides an outlet for self-expression and creativity but also fosters a sense of purpose and vitality. Whether it's painting, gardening, writing, or dancing, women prioritize activities that nourish their souls and replenish their spirits, enhancing their overall sense of well-being and fulfillment.

Sarah's Story

Sarah had always been a hard worker. In her 20s, she was determined to build a successful career, often working long hours as she climbed the corporate ladder. By her 30s, she had achieved many of her professional goals but often felt something was missing. She was constantly busy and stressed, struggling to balance her work and personal life.

As Sarah approached her 40s, she began to reassess her priorities. She realized that while her career was important, it wasn't the only thing that defined her. She started to make small changes in her life, prioritizing her well-being and personal happiness.

One of the first steps Sarah took was to reduce her work hours. She negotiated a more flexible schedule with her employer, allowing her to spend more time with her family and friends. This change brought her immense joy, as she was able to be present for her children's milestones and reconnect with her husband.

Sarah also pursued hobbies she had long neglected. She rediscovered her love for painting and joined a local art class. This creative outlet became a source of relaxation and inspiration, allowing her to express herself in new ways. She made new friends in the class, expanding her social circle with like-minded individuals.

In her 40s, Sarah also focused on her health and wellness. She started practicing yoga and meditation, which helped her manage stress and cultivate a sense of inner peace. She became more mindful of her diet and began cooking nutritious meals for her family, which improved their overall well-being.

With these changes, Sarah found a new sense of balance and fulfillment. Her career was still important to her, but it no longer dominated her life. She felt more connected to herself and her loved ones, and she was able to enjoy the present moment without constantly worrying about the future.

By the time she reached her mid-40s, Sarah felt a profound

sense of life satisfaction. She was content with the woman she had become and grateful for the experiences that had shaped her journey. She knew that life would continue to bring challenges, but she felt equipped to handle them with grace and resilience.

Sarah's 40s were a time of transformation and self-discovery. She embraced this decade with open arms, finding joy in the everyday moments and appreciating the richness of her life. Her story is a testament to the power of prioritizing one's own happiness and the fulfillment that can come from living a balanced, authentic life.

Chapter 6

Relationship Maturity

Relationship Maturity

"A woman's relationship with herself is the most important relationship she will ever have. It takes years to grow into your true self, but once you do, every relationship in your life will benefit from that maturity." - Maya Angelou

Women embody a remarkable sense of relationship maturity, characterized by self-awareness, empathy, and effective communication in their 40's. As they cultivate deeper connections with their partners, they prioritize mutual respect, support, and shared growth, fostering bonds that withstand the test of time. Through their journey of self-discovery and relational evolution, women in their 40s embrace the richness of mature relationships, finding fulfillment, joy, and companionship along the way.

Women often find themselves at a unique juncture in their personal lives, where experiences, insights, and self-awareness converge to shape their approach to relationships. This essay explores the concept of relationship maturity in women during this transformative decade, examining the evolution of emotional intelligence, communication skills, and relational dynamics that contribute to flourishing bonds.

Self-Awareness and Emotional Intelligence

In the 40s, women embark on a journey of self-discovery marked by heightened self-awareness and emotional intelligence, enriching their relationships with depth and insight. Through self-reflection, women in their 40s cultivate a deeper understanding of their values, needs, and aspirations, laying the groundwork for meaningful connections with others. Having weathered life's ups and downs, women develop emotional resilience, equipping them with the strength and insight to navigate relationship challenges with grace and poise.

Furthermore, the 40s bring an enhanced capacity for empathy and compassion, fostering deeper connections and richer interactions in relationships. Women attune to their partner's emotions and perspectives, offering a supportive presence and a listening ear. Prioritizing compassionate communication, women express empathy and understanding even in moments of conflict or disagreement, nurturing an environment of trust and mutual respect.

Communication and Conflict Resolution

Effective communication lies at the heart of mature relationships, fostering intimacy, understanding, and connection. In the 40s, women prioritize open dialogue, creating a safe space where partners can freely express their thoughts, feelings, and concerns. They hone their listening skills, engaging actively with their partner's viewpoints and fostering deeper connections through attentive listening and empathetic responses.

Moreover, conflict resolution becomes a collaborative endeavor guided by emotional intelligence and mutual respect. Rather than avoiding conflict, mature women approach disagreements as opportunities for growth and understanding, seeking mutually beneficial resolutions that strengthen the bond between partners. Harnessing emotional regulation skills, women maintain composure during conflicts, fostering constructive dialogue and preserving relationship harmony.

Prioritizing Partnership

In mature relationships, mutual respect and support form the cornerstone of partnership dynamics. Women in their 40s prioritize nurturing a sense of partnership and collaboration, respecting each other's autonomy, goals, and boundaries. They provide and receive emotional support from their partners, creating a nurturing environment for growth and fulfillment.

Furthermore, the 40s bring an enhanced capacity for empathy and compassion, fostering deeper connections and richer interactions in relationships. Women attune to their partner's emotions and perspectives, offering a supportive presence and a listening ear. Prioritizing compassionate communication, women express empathy and understanding even in moments of conflict or disagreement, nurturing an environment of trust and mutual respect.

How you can foster relationship maturity in your 40s

Cultivating relationship maturity in one's 40s involves a deliberate and introspective approach to personal growth and relational dynamics. Here are some ways women can foster relationship maturity during this transformative decade:

1. Self-Reflection and Awareness: Spend time introspecting about your values, needs, and communication style. Understanding yourself better allows you to approach relationships with clarity and authenticity.

2. Effective Communication: Hone your communication skills by actively listening, expressing yourself clearly, and practicing empathy. Open, honest communication fosters understanding and trust in relationships.

3. Emotional Intelligence: Develop emotional resilience and regulation skills to gracefully navigate conflicts and challenges. Recognize and manage your emotions while empathizing with others' perspectives.

4. Boundaries and Self-Care: Establish healthy boundaries to protect your well-being and maintain autonomy within relationships. Prioritize self-care activities that replenish your energy and foster a sense of balance.

5. Conflict Resolution: Learn constructive ways to address conflicts and disagreements, focusing on finding mutually beneficial solutions rather than escalating tensions.

6. Empathy and Compassion: Cultivate empathy and compassion towards yourself and others, recognizing that everyone has their own struggles and perspectives. Approach interactions with kindness and understanding.

7. Mutual Respect and Support: Foster mutual respect and support in relationships by valuing each other's opinions, choices, and autonomy. Celebrate each other's achievements and encourage challenges.

8. Forgiveness and Acceptance: Practice forgiveness and acceptance, both towards yourself and others. Let go of past grievances and embrace imperfections, allowing room for growth and understanding.

9. Continuous Learning and Growth: Stay open to learning and personal growth within your relationships. Embrace new experiences, perspectives, and challenges as opportunities for mutual development and enrichment.

10. Prioritize Quality Connections: Focus on nurturing meaningful, authentic connections rather than quantity. Invest time and effort into relationships that bring positivity, fulfillment, and mutual growth.

By integrating these practices into their lives, women can cultivate relationship maturity in their 40s, fostering deeper connections, understanding, and fulfillment in their interpersonal interactions.

Chapter 7

Nurturing Friendships

Nurturing Friendships

"A woman's friendship is like a garden, carefully nurtured and tended to with love, trust, and understanding. These bonds, cultivated over time, bloom into lifelong connections that provide support, joy, and a sense of belonging.~ Unknown"

Friendships take on a renewed significance in women in their 40s, evolving into essential pillars of support, companionship, and personal growth. This exploration delves into the intricate dynamics of friendships among women in their 40s, delving into their importance, the evolving nature of these connections, and strategies for nurturing enduring and meaningful relationships.

The Importance of Friendships

Friendships in a woman's 40s serve as lifelines in times of need, offering a vital source of emotional support and understanding during challenging life transitions. Whether navigating career changes, relationship challenges, or personal struggles, friends provide a comforting presence, empathy, and a listening ear, helping women navigate the complexities of life with grace and resilience. Moreover, friendships become vessels for celebrating achievements, milestones, and joys, enriching women's lives, and fostering a sense of connection and belonging within their social circles.

Evolving Dynamics

As women navigate their 40s, friendships evolve naturally, adapting to shifting priorities and changing circumstances. Juggling multiple roles and responsibilities, women in their 40s seek understanding and flexibility from their friends, recognizing the importance of balancing personal and professional commitments. Friendships adapt to changing needs and circumstances, with women prioritizing quality over quantity in their social circles, cultivating more profound connections with those who share their values, interests, and life experiences.

Challenges and Strategies

Challenges such as time constraints and busy schedules can hinder maintaining solid friendships in women's 40s. Intentional efforts are required to overcome scheduling challenges and stay connected, with women prioritizing meaningful interactions over frequency. Honest and open communication fosters trust and intimacy in friendships, allowing women to navigate conflicts and misunderstandings gracefully and understanding. Reciprocity and mutual support are also essential in sustaining friendships, with women offering a listening ear, practical assistance, and emotional validation to each other, strengthening the bonds of friendship even amidst life's challenges.

Fostering New Connections

In nurturing friendships in their 40s, women seek out shared interests, hobbies, and passions as common ground for forging new connections. Whether through book clubs, fitness classes, or community groups, women engage in activities that align with their interests, enriching their lives and expanding their social circles. Involvement in community engagement activities provides further opportunities for women to connect with like-minded individuals, fostering new friendships based on shared values and a sense of belonging.

In essence, friendships in a woman's 40s are characterized by their depth, resilience, and authenticity, serving as essential sources of support, companionship, and personal growth. By navigating the evolving dynamics of friendships with grace and intentionality, women cultivate enduring connections that enrich their lives and contribute to their overall sense of well-being and fulfillment.

Friendships are a cornerstone of well-being and fulfillment for women in their 40s, offering companionship, support, and shared experiences. By navigating the challenges of busy schedules, evolving priorities, and changing dynamics with resilience and intentionality, women cultivate enduring friendships that enrich their lives and sustain them through life's joys and challenges. As they continue to nurture connections old and new, women in their 40s embrace the power of friendship as a source of strength, joy, and belonging.

Emma's Story

Emma had always been the glue that held her family together. With two teenage children, a demanding job as a project manager, and a husband who frequently traveled for work, her days were filled with endless responsibilities. As she approached her 40s, Emma began to feel a deep yearning for connection beyond the walls of her home and office. She realized that amidst the hustle and bustle, she had neglected her friendships.

Determined to change this, Emma decided to reconnect with old friends and forge new relationships. She started by reaching out to Sarah, her college roommate, who lived just a few miles away. They had lost touch over the years but quickly rekindled their bond over coffee dates and weekend hikes. Their conversations, filled with laughter and shared memories, became a source of immense joy and comfort for Emma.

Encouraged by this, Emma joined a local book club. It was there that she met Lisa, a spirited woman with a passion for literature and life. Their shared love for books sparked a beautiful friendship. They spent hours discussing their favorite reads, often losing track of time. Lisa's zest for life was infectious, and Emma found herself embracing new hobbies and interests.

Emma also decided to volunteer at a community center, where she met Maria, a warm-hearted woman with a knack for bringing people together. Maria introduced Emma to a circle of women who met weekly to support each other through life's ups and downs. These meetings became a sanctuary for Emma, a place where she could share her fears, dreams, and triumphs without judgment.

As Emma nurtured these friendships, she noticed a profound change in herself. She felt more grounded, more at peace, and more fulfilled than she had in years. Her friends became her pillars of support, celebrating her successes and providing solace during challenging times. They taught her the value of vulnerability and the strength that comes from genuine connections.

One memorable evening, Emma hosted a dinner party for her friends. As they gathered around the table, sharing stories and laughter, she felt an overwhelming sense of gratitude. She realized that nurturing these friendships had enriched her life in ways she had never imagined. Her 40s, once feared as a time of inevitable decline, had become a decade of growth, joy, and deep, meaningful connections.

Emma's story is a testament to the power of friendship and

the fulfillment it brings, especially in the middle years of life. Through her experiences, she learned that nurturing and cherishing the bonds that truly matter is never too late.

Being selective about friends is important for maintaining healthy and fulfilling relationships. Here are some steps to help you choose friends wisely:

1. Reflect on Your Values and Interests
   - Identify what is important to you in life, such as honesty, kindness, ambition, or a sense of humor.
   - Consider hobbies and activities you enjoy to find people with similar interests.

2. Observe Their Behavior
   - Notice how potential friends treat others, including those who can't offer them anything in return.
   - Look for consistency in their actions and words over time.

3. Evaluate the Quality of Interaction
   - Pay attention to how you feel after spending time with them. Do you feel uplifted or drained?
   - Assess whether they show genuine interest in you and your well-being.

4. Set Boundaries
   - Be clear about your limits and see if they respect them.
   - A healthy friendship respects personal boundaries and doesn't push you into uncomfortable situations.

5. Look for Mutual Respect and Support
 - A good friend respects your opinions, even if they differ, and supports your goals.
 - Seek friends who celebrate your successes and provide comfort during tough times.

6. Assess Their Reliability
 - Determine if they keep their promises and can be depended upon in times of need.
 - Reliability is a key component of trust in any relationship.

7. Consider Their Influence on You
 - Reflect on whether they encourage positive behavior and growth.
 - Avoid those who bring out negative traits or habits in you.

8. Trust Your Instincts
 - If something feels off about a person, pay attention to that feeling.
 - Your intuition can often sense red flags that your conscious mind might miss.

9. Look for Reciprocity
 - Ensure that the friendship is balanced, with both parties giving and receiving support and affection.
 - One-sided relationships can lead to burnout and resentment.

10. Evaluate Their Long-term Compatibility

 - Consider if you can see this person being a positive part of your life for years to come.

 - Think about shared goals, lifestyles, and values for long-term compatibility.

By being mindful of these factors, you can build a circle of friends who enhance your life and contribute to your well-being.

Chapter 8

Parenting

Parenting

"Parenting in your 40s combines wisdom and experience, demanding a balance of energy and patience as you grow alongside your children." ~ Queenkay

For women in their 40s, parenting signifies a unique journey imbued with a blend of experience, maturity, and a profound sense of purpose.

1. Embracing Motherhood

Women in their 40s approach motherhood with a seasoned perspective, drawing upon past parenting experiences and life lessons to navigate the complexities of raising children. This seasoned parenthood imbues women with a sense of confidence and wisdom, allowing them to approach their role as mothers with self-assuredness and acceptance. With age comes a greater trust in their instincts and an enhanced ability to make informed decisions that serve the best interests of their children.

2. Navigating Family Dynamics

In their 40s, women navigate the intricate web of multi-generational relationships, balancing the needs of their children with those of aging parents or extended family members. Bridging generations fosters a sense of continuity, heritage, and mutual support within the family unit.

Building strong connections between children and grandparents cultivates a rich tapestry of intergenerational bonding, enriching family dynamics and providing a supportive network for all members.

3. Career and Parenting

Balancing career aspirations with parental responsibilities is a hallmark of parenthood in one's 40s. Women navigate the delicate dance of work-life integration, seeking flexible work arrangements and supportive environments that accommodate their roles as both professionals and parents. Leading by example, women model work ethic, resilience, and passion in their careers, instilling valuable lessons in their children and empowering them to pursue their aspirations with diligence and perseverance.

4. Parenthood and Self-Care

Amidst the demands of parenthood, women prioritize their well-being through self-care practices that sustain their mental, emotional, and physical health. Recognizing the importance of carving out time for relaxation, exercise, and personal pursuits, women demonstrate resilience and self-care habits that teach their children the importance of prioritizing their own well-being. Role modeling resilience and self-care fosters lifelong habits of well-being and empowers children to navigate life's challenges with strength and grace.

5. Reflection and Growth

Parenthood in one's 40s serves as a catalyst for personal development and growth, prompting women to embark on a journey of continuous learning and self-discovery. Drawing from their experiences as parents, women evolve as individuals, finding fulfillment and a sense of purpose beyond their roles as mothers. Balancing the demands of parenthood with personal aspirations and interests enables women to embrace the richness of life and chart a path of growth, reflection, and fulfillment.

Claire's Story

Claire had always imagined having children in her 30s, but life had other plans. After building a successful career and traveling the world, she finally felt ready to settle down and start a family. At 42, Claire gave birth to her daughter, Emily.

Parenting in her 40s brought unique challenges and rewards. Claire navigated the sleepless nights and early mornings with a sense of gratitude and patience she might not have had in her younger years. Her life experiences had equipped her with resilience and a deep appreciation for the small, everyday moments with Emily.

Claire often marveled at how much she had changed since her 20s and 30s. Back then, she had been consumed by ambition and the desire to prove herself. Now, she found joy in the simple acts of reading bedtime stories, baking cookies, and exploring the world through Emily's eyes.

Her friends, many of whom had children in their 20s and 30s, often remarked on Claire's calm demeanor and ability to handle the ups and downs of parenting with grace. Claire attributed this to the wisdom she had gained over the years. She was less concerned with perfection and more focused on being present for her daughter.

One summer evening, as Claire and Emily sat on their porch watching the sunset, Claire felt a profound sense of contentment. She knew that her journey to motherhood had been different from many others, but it was perfect for her. In her 40s, Claire had found a balance between career, personal growth, and family that brought her immense satisfaction.

Parenting in her 40s had been an unexpected adventure, but it had also been the most fulfilling chapter of her life. Claire looked forward to the years ahead, confident in her ability to guide and support Emily with the love and wisdom she had cultivated over the years.

Chapter 9

Godliness

Godliness

"Godliness is the foundation of a good life, reflecting divine virtues in everyday actions.." ~
Pastor Bola A

In a woman's 40's, the journey towards godliness represents a decade of profound transformation, characterized by spiritual growth, inner reflection, and alignment with higher principles. This pivotal stage allows women to deepen their connection with their faith and cultivate virtues such as compassion, gratitude, and humility.

During this transformative decade, women often reassess their values and priorities, seeking greater meaning and purpose in their lives. They may embark on a spiritual quest, exploring different religious or philosophical traditions or deepening their commitment to their existing faith practices. Through prayer, meditation, and contemplation, women in their 40s delve into the depths of their souls, seeking guidance and wisdom from divine sources.

As they journey towards godliness, women in their 40s cultivate a sense of reverence and awe for the wonders of creation and the mysteries of existence. They recognize the interconnectedness of all living beings and strive to live in harmony with the natural world. Through acts of kindness, service, and charity, they express their devotion to God and their commitment to serving others with love and compassion.

The 40s also offer women an opportunity to confront and transcend their ego-driven desires and attachments. They learn to surrender to a higher power and trust in divine providence, relinquishing control over outcomes and embracing the divine plan for their lives. Through surrender and submission, they find peace and serenity amidst life's uncertainties and challenges.

This decade of transformation is also marked by a deepening sense of gratitude and appreciation for life's blessings. Women in their 40s learn to count their blessings and cultivate an attitude of thankfulness for the abundance that surrounds them. They recognize the divine hand at work in every aspect of their lives and offer prayers of gratitude for the gift of existence.

As they journey towards godliness, women in their 40s also strive to embody divine virtues in their daily lives. They seek to emulate the qualities of compassion, forgiveness, and kindness, extending love and grace to all beings. Through their words and actions, they become beacons of light and agents of healing in a world in need of spiritual nourishment.

In essence, the 40s represent a decade of spiritual

awakening and transformation for women, as they deepen their connection with the divine and strive to embody godliness in their thoughts, words, and deeds.

Through prayer, meditation, and acts of service, they cultivate a profound sense of inner peace, joy, and fulfillment that transcends worldly concerns and elevates them to a higher plane of existence.

Culturing godliness in women in their 40s involves nurturing a deep spiritual connection and embodying values of compassion, integrity, and service. Here are several ways in which women in their 40s can foster godliness in their lives:

Women in their 40s often foster godliness through various practices and approaches reflecting maturity and life experiences. Here are some ways they might do so:

1. Deepening Spiritual Practices: Engaging in regular prayer, meditation, and scripture reading to cultivate a closer relationship with God.

2. Community Involvement: Participating in or leading church activities, Bible studies, and spiritual retreats to foster community and support.

3. Mentorship: Guiding and mentoring younger women in their spiritual journeys, sharing wisdom and experiences

gained over the years.

4. Living by Example: Demonstrating godly values such as kindness, patience, and integrity in daily life, serving as a role model for others.

5. Service and Charity: Volunteering and contributing to charitable causes, reflecting God's love through acts of service and compassion.

6. Continuous Learning: Engaging in theological studies, reading spiritual books, and attending workshops to deepen their understanding of faith.

7. Family Leadership: Leading their families in spiritual practices, fostering an environment where faith is nurtured and discussed openly.

8. Self-Care and Balance: Practicing self-care to maintain physical, emotional, and spiritual well-being, recognizing the importance of a balanced life in serving God effectively.

These practices help women in their 40s to foster a deeper sense of godliness, contributing positively to their personal growth and the well-being of those around them.

Julia's Story

At 42, Julia found herself in the thick of life's demands. With two teenagers navigating high school, an aging mother who needed care, and a full-time job as a nurse, she often felt overwhelmed. Amidst the chaos, she sought solace in her faith, hoping to find peace and direction.

Julia had always been spiritual, but her 40s brought a deeper yearning to connect with God. One Sunday, she attended a women's retreat organized by her church. The theme was "Experiencing Godliness in Every Season of Life." Skeptical yet hopeful, Julia went, seeking something to rejuvenate her weary soul.

The retreat was transformative. Surrounded by women of all ages, Julia listened to stories of struggle and triumph. She participated in workshops on prayer, meditation, and scripture study. One session, led by an elderly woman named Ruth, particularly touched her. Ruth spoke about the power of godliness in everyday actions, emphasizing kindness, patience, and service.

Julia realized that fostering godliness didn't require grand gestures. It was in the small, consistent acts of love and faith. She started incorporating these lessons into her daily life. She woke up early to pray and meditate, finding that these quiet moments gave her strength for the day ahead. At work, she began seeing her patients not just as tasks to be completed, but as individuals in need of compassion. She listened more intently, offered words of comfort, and prayed silently for them.

At home, Julia's new approach began to bear fruit. She started a weekly family prayer night, where they shared their thoughts and prayed together. Her teenagers, initially resistant, began to open up, and the family grew closer. Julia also made time to visit her mother regularly, bringing her meals and spending quality time together.

One evening, as Julia sat on her porch, watching the sunset, she reflected on the past year. She felt a profound sense of peace and fulfillment. Despite the challenges, she had found a way to weave godliness into the fabric of her daily life. The chaos was still there, but it was now interwoven with moments of grace and divine presence.

Julia realized that experiencing godliness was not about escaping life's difficulties but finding God within them. Her faith had deepened, her relationships had strengthened, and she had discovered a wellspring of inner peace that she could draw from every day.

In her 40s, Julia found that godliness was not a destination but a journey—a daily practice of living out her faith in the midst of life's beautiful messiness. And in this journey, she discovered the true essence of grace.

Chapter 10

Authentic Self

Authentic Self

I Became More Comfortable with Who I Am, Always My Authentic Self.
~ Crystal Wright, Attorney

In a woman's 40s, the pursuit of authenticity emerges as a central theme, marking a transformative journey toward self-discovery and empowerment. This pivotal decade offers women an opportunity to peel back the layers of societal expectations and external pressures to reveal the true essence of who they are.

Amidst the complexities of midlife, women in their 40s embark on a quest to reclaim their authentic selves, embracing their unique strengths, passions, and vulnerabilities. They confront the narratives of their past and redefine their identities on their own terms, liberated from the constraints of conformity and comparison.

The pursuit of authenticity is characterized by a deepening sense of self-awareness—a profound understanding of one's values, beliefs, and aspirations. Women in their 40s engage in introspection and reflection, gaining insights into their innermost desires and motivations.

As they embrace their authentic selves, women in their 40s cultivate a sense of confidence and self-assurance that emanates from within.

They learn to trust their intuition and honor their inner voice, embracing the wisdom that arises from their lived experiences.

Authenticity also involves embracing vulnerability and imperfection as integral aspects of the human experience. Women in their 40s learn to embrace their flaws and limitations, viewing them not as weaknesses but as opportunities for growth and self-compassion.

The pursuit of authenticity is inseparable from the practice of self-care and self-love. Women prioritize their well-being and nourish their bodies, minds, and spirits through practices such as mindfulness, self-compassion, and self-expression.

Authenticity extends beyond individual identity to encompass the cultivation of meaningful and fulfilling relationships. Women in their 40s seek connections with others based on mutual respect, understanding, and acceptance.

As they embrace their authentic selves, women in their 40s find the courage to set boundaries and assert their needs and desires in personal and professional relationships. They refuse to compromise their values or sacrifice their authenticity for the sake of external validation.

The pursuit of authenticity is a dynamic and evolving process that unfolds over time. Women in their 40s recognize that authenticity is not a destination but a journey —a continual process of self-discovery, growth, and evolution.

Authenticity is also about living in alignment with one's values and aspirations. Women in their 40s make conscious choices that reflect their true selves, whether it's pursuing a new career path, engaging in creative pursuits, or advocating for causes they believe in.

Pursuing authenticity involves embracing change and the fullness of life's experiences. Women in their 40s navigate transitions and challenges with grace and resilience, trusting in their inner strength and resilience.

As they embrace their authentic selves, women in their 40s find liberation from the need for external validation or approval. They recognize that true fulfillment comes from within and prioritize their own happiness and well-being above all else.

Authenticity is also about embracing the journey of self-discovery with curiosity and openness. Women in their 40s approach life with a sense of wonder and adventure, embracing new opportunities and experiences with enthusiasm and optimism.

The pursuit of authenticity involves letting go of outdated beliefs or expectations that no longer serve them. Women in their 40s release self-imposed limitations and embrace the limitless possibilities that await them.

Authenticity is about embracing one's passions and interests without fear or reservation. Women in their 40s pursue their dreams with gusto, unapologetically following their hearts and expressing their true selves.

As they embrace their authentic selves, women in their 40s cultivate a deep sense of gratitude for the journey that has brought them to this moment. They cherish the lessons learned and the growth experienced along the way.

The pursuit of authenticity is also about finding joy and fulfillment in the present moment. Women in their 40s savor life's simple pleasures and cultivate a sense of contentment and peace within themselves.

Authenticity is about living with integrity and authenticity in all aspects of life. Women in their 40s align their actions with their values, making choices that honor their true selves and contribute to the greater good.

In essence, the pursuit of authenticity is a transformative journey that empowers women in their 40s to live authentically, boldly, and unapologetically.

As women embrace their true selves, they find liberation, fulfillment, and a renewed sense of purpose and meaning in life.

Emily's Story

At 42, Emily found herself at a crossroads. Motherhood, career, and community responsibilities had kept her busy for years, yet something within her longed for more— something she couldn't quite name. It wasn't until a quiet afternoon, sitting alone in a cozy café, that she began to listen to that inner voice.

Emily had always been a planner, her days meticulously scheduled. But on this day, she decided to take a break from the routine. Sipping her tea, she allowed her mind to wander. Memories from her youth, dreams she had set aside, and passions she had ignored flooded back. She realized how much of her authentic self she had hidden behind roles and expectations.

Determined to reconnect with herself, Emily started small. She revisited her love for painting, a hobby she had abandoned in college. Each brushstroke brought her immense joy, reminding her of the creative spirit she once embraced. She found solace in the quiet moments of creating art, feeling a piece of her soul reawaken.

Emily also started journaling, pouring out her thoughts and feelings onto the pages. This practice became a mirror, reflecting her true desires and fears. Through her writing, she discovered a deep longing for connection—not just with others, but with herself. She wanted to live a life that was genuinely hers, not merely a series of obligations.

As she continued this journey, Emily made a conscious effort to set boundaries. She learned to say no to things that drained her energy and yes to those that enriched her spirit. She reconnected with old friends who appreciated her for who she truly was and sought new experiences that aligned with her passions.

One evening, while watching the sunset from her backyard, Emily felt a profound sense of peace. She had begun to reclaim her authentic self, embracing the woman she had become. It wasn't always easy, but the journey was profoundly rewarding. In embracing her true self, Emily found a renewed sense of purpose and joy, ready to face the world with an open heart and a fearless spirit.

For the first time in years, Emily felt truly alive. She had discovered that the key to happiness lay not in fulfilling others' expectations, but in honoring her own. And in doing so, she became a beacon of authenticity for those around her, inspiring them to embark on their own journeys of self-discovery.

Chapter 11

Embracing Serenity

Embracing Serenity

"May God Grant me the Serenity to accept what I cannot change."
~ The Serenity Prayer

As women transition into their 40s, they embark on a journey toward cultivating a sense of peace, balance, and fulfillment amidst life's complexities. This exploration delves into strategies for embracing drama-free and stress-free living in this transformative decade, focusing on mindfulness, self-care, boundary-setting, and resilience-building practices.

Mindfulness and Present Moment Awareness

Women in their 40s embrace mindfulness as a pathway to presence, awareness, and inner peace. They prioritize mindful living, grounding themselves in the present moment amid life's hustle and bustle. Through mindfulness practices such as meditation, deep breathing, and body scans, women manage stress, anxiety, and overwhelm, fostering a calmer, more centered state of being.

As they embrace their authentic selves, women in their 40s cultivate a sense of confidence and self-assurance that emanates from within.

Self-Care and Prioritizing Well-being

Holistic self-care takes precedence as women prioritize activities that nourish their physical, emotional, and spiritual well-being. From regular exercise and healthy eating to adequate sleep and relaxation techniques, women nurture their bodies and minds with care and intention.

Learning to say no to commitments that drain their energy or compromise their well-being empowers women to prioritize self-care and maintain healthy boundaries. Engaging in hobbies and activities that bring joy, fulfillment, and a sense of accomplishment enriches women's lives and fosters a balanced perspective. Furthermore, women seek avenues for making meaningful contributions to their communities, careers, or causes that resonate with their values and passions.

Setting Boundaries and Managing Relationships

Clear communication and assertiveness are pivotal in navigating relationships with grace and authenticity. Women in their 40s assert their needs, preferences, and boundaries clearly and confidently, fostering healthy, mutually respectful relationships. Addressing conflicts with openness, empathy, and assertiveness enables women to navigate relationship challenges constructively without resorting to drama or negativity. Surrounding themselves with supportive, uplifting relationships that nurture their well-being, and a sense of belonging become priorities. Recognizing and releasing toxic relationships or dynamics frees women from unnecessary drama and stress, creating space for healthier connections and personal growth.

Women in their 40s embrace a lifestyle characterized by serenity, resilience, and authenticity. They navigate life's complexities with grace and equanimity by prioritizing mindfulness, self-care, boundary-setting, and nurturing positive relationships. Through conscious choices and intentional living, women in their 40s cultivate a drama-free and stress-free existence, embracing the fullness of life with a sense of peace, balance, and fulfillment.

Joy's Story

Joy, a woman in her 40s, had always been busy. Juggling her demanding career as a lawyer, raising two children, and managing her household left little room for anything else. She was known for her efficiency, always on top of her responsibilities, but it came at a cost. As the years passed, Joy became increasingly overwhelmed by stress and fatigue. The constant rush, the unending list of tasks, and the pressure to meet everyone's expectations had worn her down.

One day, after a particularly grueling week, Joy looked at herself in the mirror and barely recognized the woman staring back at her. The stress lines on her face, the tiredness in her eyes—she realized that she had been running on empty for too long. She knew something had to change. That weekend, she decided to step back from her usual routine and spend some time alone. She drove to a quiet cabin in the mountains, away from the hustle and bustle of her daily life. The peace and solitude were refreshing, and for the first time in years, Joy allowed herself just to be.

As she sat on the porch, listening to the birds and watching the trees sway in the breeze, Joy began to reflect on her life. She realized that she had been so focused on achieving external success and fulfilling others' expectations that she had neglected her own well-being. The constant striving had left her disconnected from herself, her passions, and what truly brought her joy. In the stillness of that moment, Joy made a decision. She would no longer let stress dictate her life. She would embrace serenity and prioritize her own peace of mind.

Returning home, Joy began to make changes. She started practicing mindfulness, meditating for a few minutes daily, focusing on her breath, and grounding herself in the present moment. This simple practice brought her a sense of calm she hadn't felt in years. Joy also learned to say no to unnecessary commitments, toxic relationships, and anything that drained her energy. She set clear boundaries, ensuring that her time was respected and her well-being prioritized.

Her relationships improved as well. With her newfound serenity, Joy was more present, patient, and loving with her children. She no longer snapped at them out of frustration but listened to them with an open heart. Her relationship with her husband deepened as they spent more quality time together, reconnecting on a level they hadn't been on in years.

Joy remained committed and successful at work, but she no longer allowed her career to consume her. She balanced her professional life with her personal needs, delegating tasks when necessary and avoiding burnout. She advocated for well-being in her office, encouraging her colleagues to take care of themselves as well.

Joy's journey towards serenity was ongoing, but she embraced it fully. She knew that life would always have its challenges, but she now faced them with a sense of calm and resilience that she had never had before. By prioritizing her peace, Joy discovered a deeper, more meaningful way of living—one that nourished her soul and allowed her to flourish in every aspect of her life.

Chapter 12

Physical and Mental Well-being

Physical and Mental Wellbeing

"To keep the body in good health is a duty. Otherwise, we shall be unable to keep our mind strong and clear." ~ Buddha

In a woman's 40s, the well-being landscape undergoes a profound transformation, marked by a confluence of physical and mental changes influenced by internal and external factors. From hormonal fluctuations to societal expectations, women in their 40s navigate a complex terrain, seeking equilibrium in both body and mind. This exploration delves into the multifaceted physical and mental well-being dimensions during this significant phase of a woman's life.

Physical Well-being

The onset of perimenopause heralds a period of hormonal changes characterized by irregular periods, hot flashes, and mood swings as women transition toward menopause. With the cessation of menstruation, hormonal shifts impact various bodily functions, including metabolism, bone density, and cardiovascular health.

As metabolism tends to slow down in the 40s, weight management becomes more challenging, necessitating strategies such as balanced nutrition and regular exercise. Additionally, the risk of chronic conditions like diabetes, hypertension, and cardiovascular disease increases, underscoring the importance of preventive healthcare measures. Maintaining bone health is paramount, with declining estrogen levels contributing to decreased bone density and heightened susceptibility to osteoporosis. Adequate calcium intake, vitamin D supplementation, and weight-bearing exercises play a crucial role in preserving bone health. Embracing strength training exercises helps preserve muscle mass and bone density, while aerobic activities improve cardiovascular health and enhance overall fitness levels.

Mental Well-being

Psychological resilience becomes paramount in navigating the myriad transitions and challenges of midlife, such as career changes, empty nesting, or caring for aging parents. Engaging in mindfulness practices, seeking social support, and cultivating a sense of purpose can bolster one's ability to cope with these changes. Hormonal fluctuations during perimenopause may exacerbate mood swings, anxiety, and depression, highlighting the importance of awareness and proactive management for maintaining emotional well-being. Prioritizing self-care activities such as adequate sleep, relaxation techniques, and creative outlets fosters emotional balance and stress resilience. Some women may experience subtle changes in cognitive function during their 40s, such as lapses in memory or difficulty concentrating. Mental stimulation through activities like reading, puzzles, or learning new skills promotes cognitive vitality. Adopting a brain-healthy lifestyle comprising a balanced diet, regular exercise, social engagement, and cognitive stimulation reduces the risk of age-related cognitive decline, ensuring mental well-being and vitality in the 40s and beyond.

In essence, navigating physical and mental well-being in one's 40s is a multi-faceted journey that requires attention, intention, and proactive management. By embracing lifestyle practices that promote health and resilience, women can thrive in this transformative decade of life.

As women transition through their 40s, nurturing physical and mental well-being becomes an integral aspect of holistic health. Embracing the changes wrought by midlife with resilience and self-compassion empowers women to thrive amidst the complexities of this transformative phase. Through mindful attention to their bodies and minds, women in their 40s embark on a journey of self-discovery and growth, forging a path toward vibrant well-being and fulfillment.

Sara's Story

At 45, Sara had reached a breaking point. Years of prioritizing work and family over herself had taken a toll on her physical and mental health. She felt perpetually exhausted, her mind foggy, and her body aching in ways never before. One morning, as she struggled to button her blouse, she saw herself in the mirror and knew something had to change.

Sara decided it was time to reclaim her health. She started with small steps, beginning with a visit to her doctor. The check-up confirmed what she already knew: she needed to make significant lifestyle changes. Armed with this knowledge, she devised a plan to focus on her physical and mental well-being.

Her first step was improving her diet. Gone were the fast-food lunches and late-night snacks. Instead, Sara embraced whole foods—fresh vegetables, lean proteins, and whole grains. She learned to cook simple, nutritious meals and discovered a new love for cooking. Each meal became an opportunity to nourish her body and soul.

Next, Sara committed to a regular exercise routine. She joined a local gym and hired a personal trainer who understood her goals and limitations. The first few sessions were tough; her muscles ached, and she often felt like giving up. But she persisted, finding joy in the gradual progress.

The endorphin rush after each workout became addictive, and soon, she looked forward to her gym sessions.

Mental health was equally important in her journey. Sara began practicing mindfulness and meditation. She found a quiet corner in her home, where she could sit in peace, focusing on her breath and letting go of the day's stresses. This daily practice helped her feel more centered and calm.

Sara also sought therapy, realizing that she needed professional help to address the anxiety and stress that had built up over the years. Her therapist provided her with tools to manage her emotions and cope with life's challenges more effectively. Through these sessions, Sara gained a deeper understanding of herself and learned to prioritize her needs without guilt.

As months passed, Sara's changes were remarkable. She lost weight, her skin glowed, and she had more energy than she had in years. But the most significant transformation was in her mindset. She felt more confident, happier, and resilient. Sara had learned to listen to her body and mind, recognizing the importance of balance in her life.

One day, while hiking a trail she once found too daunting, Sara reached the summit and gazed out at the breathtaking view. She felt a profound sense of accomplishment and gratitude. This journey of reclaiming her health had not only transformed her body but had also renewed her spirit.

She realized that taking care of herself was not a luxury but a necessity, one that empowered her to live her life to the fullest.

In embracing her physical and mental health, Sara discovered a new passion for life. She became an advocate for wellness, encouraging friends and family to embark on their own health journeys. Her story became an inspiration, showing that it's never too late to prioritize oneself and reclaim the happiness and vitality that everyone deserves.

Chapter 13

Being Intentional

Being Intentional

"Happiness is not something ready-made. It comes from your own actions.
~ Dalai Lama

Women in their 40s often find themselves at a pivotal juncture, where the blend of life experience and newfound wisdom empowers them to be more intentional in their actions and decisions. This period is characterized by a deliberate approach to various aspects of life, from career choices and personal relationships to self-care and personal growth.

One of the most significant ways women in their 40s practice intentionality is through career decisions. By this age, many have achieved substantial professional success and clarity about what truly brings them fulfillment. Rather than climbing the corporate ladder for the sake of external validation, they seek roles and projects that align with their values and passions. This shift often leads to more meaningful work experiences and a greater sense of professional satisfaction.

In their personal lives, women in their 40s are more selective about the relationships they nurture. They prioritize connections that are supportive, enriching, and reciprocal, letting go of toxic or draining relationships. This intentional approach to friendships and partnerships fosters deeper, more authentic connections, contributing to overall well-being and happiness.

Self-care becomes a deliberate practice for women in their 40s. They recognize the importance of maintaining their physical, mental, and emotional health and consciously incorporate activities that promote well-being. Whether it's regular exercise, healthy eating, mindfulness practices, or hobbies that bring joy, they understand that self-care is not a luxury but a necessity for a balanced and fulfilling life.

Intentionality also extends to personal growth and lifelong learning. Women in their 40s often seek opportunities for continued education, skill development, and new experiences. They understand that personal growth doesn't stop at a certain age and actively pursue activities that challenge them and expand their horizons. This could involve taking up new hobbies, enrolling in courses, or traveling to new places.

Family dynamics and parenting are also approached with greater intentionality. Women in their 40s strive to create meaningful family experiences and instill values that are important to them. They take deliberate steps to spend quality time with their children, partner, and extended family, fostering a strong sense of connection and support within the family unit.

Financial planning and stability also become focal points. Women in their 40s are often more financially savvy and intentional about their spending, saving, and investing.

They plan for the future, whether it's for their retirement, their children's education, or other long-term goals, ensuring financial security and peace of mind.

Moreover, being intentional in their 40s often means giving back to the community and making a positive impact. Many women volunteer, mentor younger individuals, or contribute to causes they are passionate about. This sense of purpose and contribution adds depth and meaning to their lives, reinforcing their sense of self-worth and connection to the larger world.

Finally, women in their 40s embrace intentionality in their inner lives. They seek to understand themselves better, reflecting on their past experiences, values, and beliefs. This introspection leads to greater self-awareness and a clearer sense of identity, allowing them to live more authentically and true to themselves.

In essence, women in their 40s harness the power of intentionality to create lives that are aligned with their true selves. This deliberate approach to living brings a sense of fulfillment, balance, and purpose, making this decade one of their lives' most transformative and enriching periods.

Yale's Story

Yale stood on the balcony of her downtown apartment, sipping her morning coffee as the city began to wake. At 42, she had found herself at a crossroads, a place where the cumulative experiences of her life seemed to converge, demanding intentionality and clarity.

In her twenties and thirties, Yale had been a whirlwind of activity, chasing career goals, social engagements, and personal milestones with relentless energy. But as she entered her 40s, she felt an unmistakable shift. It wasn't just the physical changes or the graying strands of hair; it was a deeper, more profound awareness that her time and energy were finite and valuable. She realized she needed to be more deliberate with her choices.

Her first intentional step was in her career. Yale had been in marketing for nearly two decades, working her way up to a senior position at a prestigious firm. While she had achieved professional success, she often felt a nagging dissatisfaction, a sense that her work was not fully aligned with her values.

After much contemplation, she decided to take a leap of faith. She left her high-paying job to start her own consultancy, focusing on sustainable and ethical brands. The decision was risky, but it reignited her passion for her work. Every project she took on felt meaningful, and she found herself more motivated and fulfilled than she had been in years.

Next, Yale turned her attention to her health. The late-night work sessions and erratic eating habits of her younger years had taken a toll. She began prioritizing her physical well-being, incorporating regular exercise, balanced nutrition, and adequate sleep into her daily routine. She discovered a love for yoga, which not only improved her physical fitness but also brought a sense of mental calm and mindfulness that she had never experienced before.

Relationships were another area where Yale chose to be intentional. She evaluated the people in her life, recognizing that some relationships had become draining and unfulfilling. With courage, she set boundaries and distanced herself from toxic friendships, choosing instead to invest in connections that were supportive and enriching. She rekindled old friendships and made new ones, surrounding herself with people who inspired and uplifted her. This change brought a profound sense of peace and happiness.

Yale also focused on her financial stability. She met with a financial advisor to create a plan that balanced her present needs with future security. This included smart investments, saving for retirement, and budgeting for her new business. By taking control of her finances, she alleviated a lot of the stress that had previously weighed on her, allowing her to focus more on her passions and less on monetary concerns.

In her quest for personal growth, Yale embraced lifelong learning. She enrolled in courses that intrigued her, from creative writing to environmental science, expanding her knowledge and skills. She started a blog to share her journey, connecting with a community of like-minded individuals and finding joy in creative expression. This ongoing education not only enriched her life but also provided new opportunities for her consultancy business.

Yale's intentional living extended to her community. She volunteered at local non-profits, using her marketing skills to help them increase their reach and impact. She mentored young women entering the business world, offering guidance and support that she had often lacked in her own early career. Giving back in these ways brought a deep sense of purpose and connection to her community.

Mindfulness became a cornerstone of Yale's daily life. She practiced meditation regularly, which helped her stay present and appreciate the small moments of joy and beauty in everyday life. This practice also improved her emotional resilience, allowing her to handle challenges with a calm and balanced approach.

Setting and achieving personal goals was another critical aspect of Yale's intentional living. She created a vision board, mapping out her aspirations in various areas of her life, from professional milestones to travel adventures. By breaking these goals into actionable steps, she made steady progress, celebrating each achievement along the way. Through it all, Yale embraced change and remained flexible. She understood that life's unpredictability required an adaptable mindset. When faced with setbacks, she viewed them as opportunities for growth and learning, continuously evolving and refining her path.

In her 40s, Yale had learned to live with intention, making choices that reflected her true self and supported her overall well-being. Her life was not just a series of tasks to be completed but a rich, fulfilling journey marked by purpose and clarity. She stood on her balcony each morning, grateful for the intentional steps she had taken and excited for the future she was actively shaping.